MW00985286

A First-Start® Easy Reader

This easy reader contains only 44 different words,
repeated often to help the young reader develop
word recognition and interest in reading.

Basic word list for *Pete the Parakeet*

the	has	going
say	bird	hello
to	when	Pete
is	says	Pete's
a	this	parakeet
and	lives	happy
he	play	chirp
my	plays	house
pet	eats	sleeps
in	bell	loves
his	open	there
on	door	swing
are	they	ring
at	where	ringing
not		friend

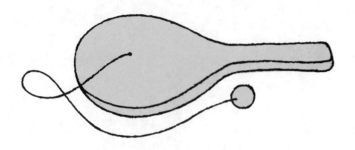

Pete
the Parakeet

Written by Sharon Gordon

Illustrated by Paul Harvey

Troll Associates

ISBN 0-89375-284-3

10 9 8 7 6 5 4

Say hello to Pete.

Pete is a parakeet.

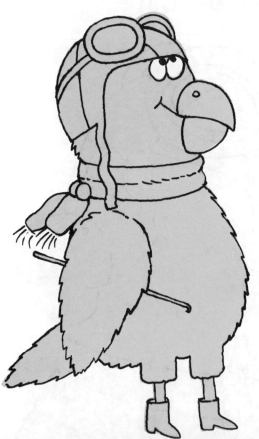

He is a bird.

He is my pet parakeet.

When Pete the parakeet is happy,

he says, "Chirp, Chirp, Chirp."

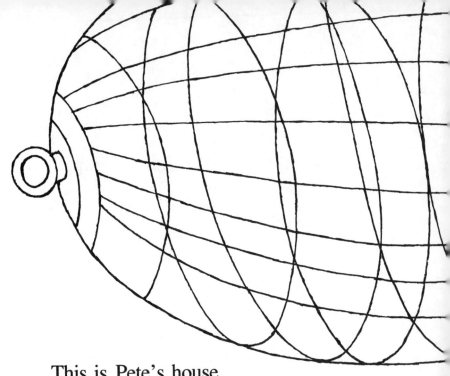

This is Pete's house.

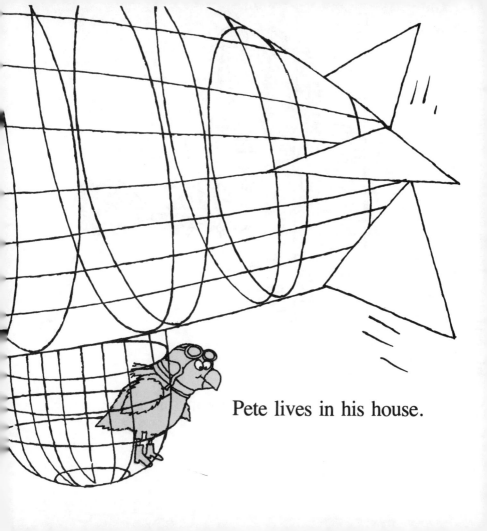

Pete lives in his house.

He plays in his house.

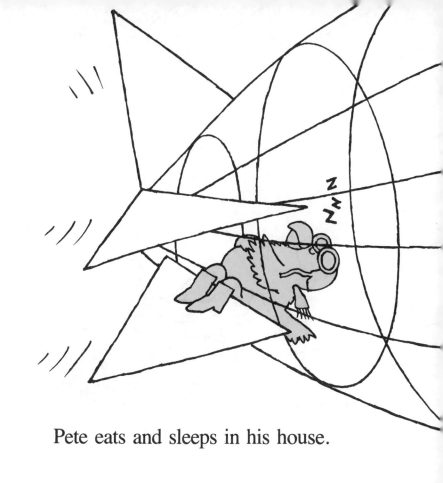

Pete eats and sleeps in his house.

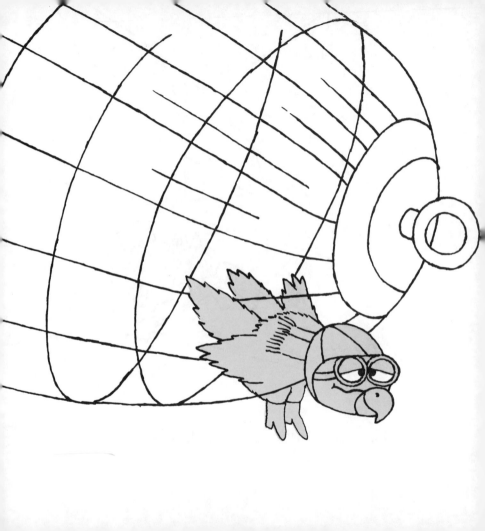

Pete loves his house.

"Chirp, Chirp, Chirp."

In Pete's house there is a swing.

Pete loves to swing.

In Pete's house there is a bell.

Pete loves to ring his bell.

RING—RING—RING!

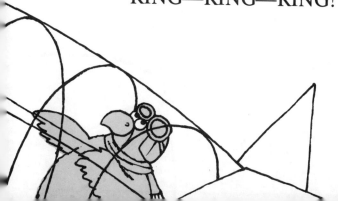

The door is open.

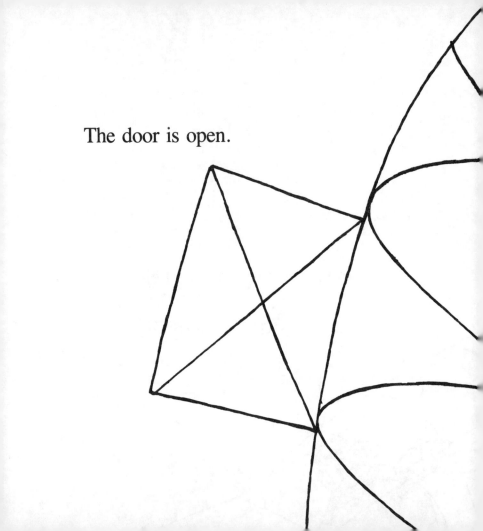

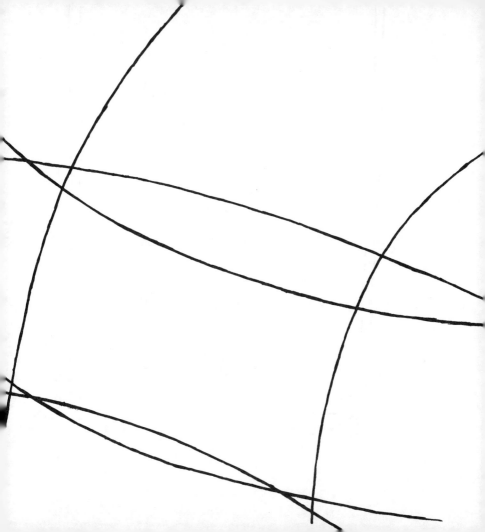

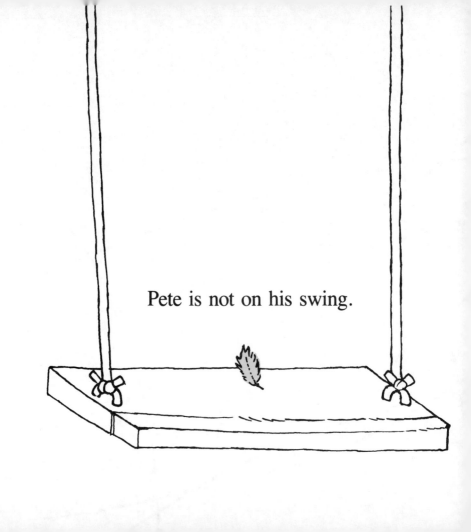

Pete is not on his swing.

He is not ringing his bell.

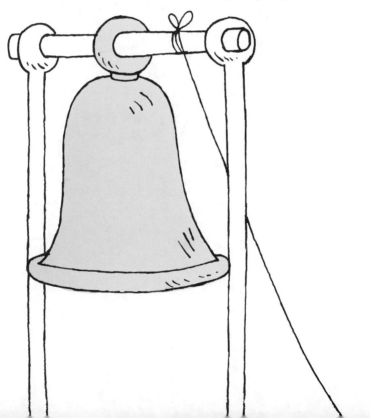

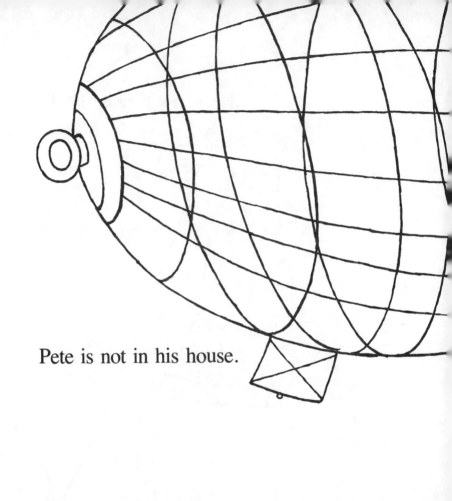

Pete is not in his house.

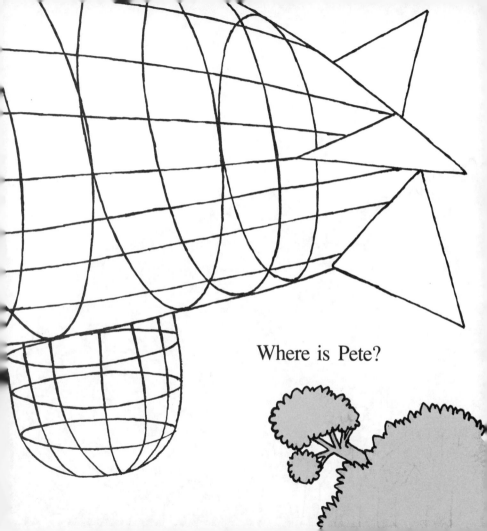

Where is Pete?

"Chirp, Chirp, Chirp."

There is Pete!

Pete has a friend.

"Chirp, Chirp, Chirp."

Where are they going?

They are going to play

at Pete's house!